The Official Guide
to the
Saving Tara
Project

Peter Bonner

The Official Guide to the Saving Tara Project
All Rights Reserved Copyright © 2014
Peter Bonner

The book is not intended to reprint all of the information available to the author or publisher on the subject, but rather to simplify, complement and supplement other available sources. The reader is encouraged to read all available material and to learn as much as possible about the subject, including www.peterbonner.com or www.savingtara.com.

For information, please address:
FirstWorks Publishing Co., Inc.
P.O. Box 93 / Marietta, GA 30061-0093
Email: firstworks@earthlink.net

Library of Congress Control Number 2014946338

ISBN: 978-0-9827994-5-1

Printed in the United State of America

The author gratefully acknowledges the following:

Photos of the movie set and actors during the production of Gone With the Wind are the property of the estate of the late Herb Bridges and are printed here by permission.

The photos of the Tara façade in 1959 just prior to its dismantling and move to Georgia are the property of Bison Archives (mailto:bisonarchives@yahoo.com) and are printed with permission.

The author greatly acknowledges the contribution and photos taken by volunteers during the work days at the Tara façade, and by those who have contributed photos from their private collection and notes that they are the sole property of those acknowledged and are printed here by permission.

Throughout this book are several quotes attributable to Margaret Mitchell's book, Gone With the Wind.

Contents

Preface

Before we go any further, I must deal with questions I have been asked by friend and foe alike since I began working on the restoration and display of the façade…"Why you?" and "Peter, how did you work this out and get permission to take on this project?"

I knew the late great Betty Talmadge for many years; in fact, I still credit her with giving me, in my opinion, one of the greatest pieces of advice for a tour site. She would tell me, "Peter, you are welcome to come and tour my home anytime you'd like, as long as you bring at least 25 friends." Ms. Betty and I were not close friends, but she never let her fame and stature stop her from taking time out to speak to me and ask me how the tours were going. And today, so many years after her death, I continue to speak of her as a leader in saving the history that now brings so many tourist dollars to metro Atlanta.

Through my association with Ms. Betty and her family, I came to meet her son Gene and her grandson Herman. It was my friendship with Gene and Herman that lead to their realization of the total tourism dollars *Gone With the Wind* is still bringing to metro Atlanta (and the South) and how the façade (and the Fitzgerald House) might fit into it. It was their personal knowledge of me and my tour that put them at ease as

Peter sorting through the large piles of lumber from the Tara façade on his first visit to the site.

to the safety and security of that which they had been made caretaker of so long ago. And, unlike the previous plans from Clayton, Fayette, Douglas, and Coweta counties, I didn't have any desire to own it or to move it. I believe the best story is found by having the Tara façade, the Fitzgerald House, and the Crawford Plantation reside together on what the Talmadge family has so long referred to as home.

So here I am….a simple story teller with the opportunity to put the most iconic of all movie sets before the world and allow those who have an interest to come and see that from which Scarlett got her strength ….Tara. And although I am currently funding this project out of my own pocket, I believe that the foundation of a great story, and thus this great tour, will not be in the look of the building, or the color of the drapes. Until such time as funds are available, the façade (and later the Fitzgerald house) will hold court in the building that served as a dairy barn and later a shelter for a refugee from the golden age of Hollywood, and the salvaged family home of a Pulitzer Prize winner.

I pray this book will serve as an encouragement to those who have a dream they seek to fulfill, those who have a project that they seek to accomplish, and those who find themselves in need of a place to call home. Tara still stands … and, until her pieces have disintegrated into the red earth of her homeland, she will continue to generate a passion in all who come under her spell.

—Peter Bonner

This project would not have begun nor the book about it completed without all the work and counsel from my wife Sharon (who simply wants her official title to be, "My Girl") and my little Sheltie, Buddy who took the role of therapy dog and my babysitter until Sharon got home. There is never a better team than family.

Dedication

As any collector, business owner, or politician can tell you, there is no guarantee that spending money will bring you fame, more business, or a seat at the political table. And yet, Betty Talmadge, antique collector, business owner, and wife of a U.S. Senator "damned the torpedoes" and moved straight ahead when she got the opportunity to rescue the Tara façade from a barn in North Georgia.

Although her vision of displaying the pieces of the façade in a custom built museum never came to fruition, it wasn't from her lack of trying. She met with representatives from at least four metro counties and listened intently to their ideas of museums, outdoor attractions and movie sets. She allowed pieces to be packed up and shipped multiple times, only to reclaim them after those suitors backed out, usually from what she would refer to as "their champagne tastes and beer pocketbook."

But Ms. Betty persisted and was able to secure the Atlanta History Center as a prime location to display the massive front entrance that was built on the Selznick back lot to welcome the guests of the O'Haras into their home. Tara, a place forever tied to the land, a place Gerald O'Hara reminded Scarlett was "worth fighting for, worth dying for; the only thing that lasts." Ms. Betty even paid the $6,000.00 cost to restore the door to its original grandeur before it was placed on display. That is how important it was to her to have this piece of Hollywood history available for all to see.

Therefore, this short guide to the quest of this author and band of volunteers to restore and present the Tara façade is dedicated to the memory of the lady who sought diligently to preserve and display a piece of Hollywood royalty. This book is dedicated to you, Ms. Betty Talmadge, with thanks and a promise to protect that which you rescued from a barn in North Georgia so that admirers the world over might make the trek to your former home and gaze upon its wrinkled but readily recognizable features. A little worn, a little faded, a little rusty, but still ready for another close up.

Bricks, Veneer and Lumber

It has been said that a great story is the soul of a presentation and so it was that a great story clothed in a little bit of brick, wood and veneer turned Tara into an icon. It is the Holy Grail for *Gone With the Wind* fans who have traversed the back roads of Georgia ever since the movie premiered in Atlanta in 1939. And even today, 75 years after it first appeared on screen, it is still touching the hearts of its longtime fans and stirring the hearts of a new generation.

But as noted, the façade from *Gone With the Wind* was just that, a façade; made not of red clay brick but of wooden scaffolding, overlaid with plywood veneer which was then covered with pressed board bricks. And the screen Tara was not situated on a hill overlooking the rolling Georgia piedmont, but rather on the 40 acre back lot of Selznick Studios in Hollywood, California.

However even after 75 years that included dedication,

This photo was taken in 1959, just prior to the façade being dismantled and removed from the Selznick Lot (then owned by Desilu Productions) for its trip to Atlanta, Georgia.

dereliction, dismantling and damage, there is still enough of the original materials from the set pieces to get an idea of its construction. On these pages are photos of the scaffolding that held together the home of the O'Haras, some up close photos of the veneering, and finally, photos of one of the few bricks remaining from the faux brick walls of Tara.

Evidence suggests the façade was built with wood scaffolding (like the 2 x 4 framed walls of a house) sheathed with a thin sheet of veneering that was the plywood of 1939. After the scaffold and

plywood were "married," the particle board (made of the same material as the brown peg board found at most building supply stores) was cut into "bricks," attached with nails, and then dressed and distressed with multiple coats of paint. It would appear this construction made the dismantling of the brick walls of Tara impractical; consequently, the windows, doors, and side porches were shipped while the faux brick walls were pushed into a pile and burned on the set. One of the few bricks remaining from Tara was found still attached to a roof cornice. The brick measures 2-1/2 inch-

es by 9-1/2 inches and is 1/4 inch thick. The front door latch plate was also made from the same material but is no more than one inch in thickness. The plywood veneer has been in the range of 2 to 2-1/2 inches thick and the framing that did survive the move has been found to be standard untreated 2 x 4 studs as well as quarter sawn boards in varying widths. Also found among the pieces are a number of "boxed" beams made to look like heavy timber, but were, in fact, three-sided and hollow so that they could be placed over the top of the standard 2 x 4 to give it the look of a large heavy beam.

(Opposite page) View inside the dairy barn home of the façade after our initial inventory (note new tags), sweeping of debris and a stacking by the volunteers. Against the wall are the large 3' 6" x 5' windows seen on the upper front of the façade. Just below them is their accompanying header. (Top left) One of the few complete Tara bricks that remain. It lies next to the piece of cornice to which it was nailed. (Middle left) This is the back of the same brick. Note the pattern of the particle board from which this brick is made. The brick measures 9-1/2 x 2-1/2 x 1/4 inches. (Bottom left) 2 x 4 fir strips were used to build the frame of Tara and to secure large pieces such as these inner shutters for the large lower windows. (Top right) A close up of brick showing their attachment to the plywood veneer which was then attached to the 2 x 4 framing.

(Top) Stacks of façade pieces after being given a new inventory tag. Volunteers assigned the same number as previous tag which was attached together. However, many of the pieces in the first inventory could not be identified and so there is still much to discover. Among the items pictured... parts of Tara's front door, shutters, cathderal window and door framing.

(Bottom left) Restoring the front window and shutter was like putting together a puzzle. This photo was taken at the very beginning of the restoration and shows how the façade was, in fact, in pieces. (Bottom right) The broken arm of a tall shutter frame. Many of the pieces were put together using a combination of mortise and tenon joints, tiny nails, small screws and Hollywood Magic.

The First Lines and the Tall Shutters

2 When the first images of Tara arrived on the screen at the premier in 1939, it was not the front door which overheard the Tarleton Twins and Scarlett arguing over whether there would be a war. Their discussion was held on the right corner of the front porch, only a few inches from the 10-foot window with its attached shutters. A window and accompanying shutters made to appear to open and close although the slates were nailed in place.

Although the shutters appear to be fully functioning, the wood rod or dowel seen above Stuart's right arm was attached to the shutter only for show, since none of the slats were moveable.

(Top) *Although distressed on set to show the ravages of war, the majority of damage to the façade appears to have happened after its arrival in Georgia. (Bottom left) This is the right side tall window seen behind Scarlett and the Twins in the opening scenes of the movie. It was identified and its provenance established by viewing photos taken before the façade was dismantled in Hollywood. (Bottom right) The shutters were built by hand and no two were exactly alike, so each slat had to be matched with the ghost of the original and reattached one by one.*

Later when Scarlett arrives home to her beloved Tara with Melanie, Prissy and baby Beau in tow, the window and massive shutters show the ravages of the war and the fighting that took place in the very yard just a few days before.

Today, the window shutter that filled the scene behind Vivian Leigh, George Reeves and Fred Crane (who spoke the first lines in this, his first movie role) still exists minus the glass panes, lower muttens and a few of the slats. The window still retains a portion of its white washed paint and the green of the shutters, now lightened by age and the brightness of the Georgia sun that has illuminated its resting place. The only restoration done to the shutter was to reattach the missing slats.

(Top right) A close look at one of the other frames shows the tiny nails or brads that were used to attach each of the slats. (Above) A stack of slats lies tied with a string unitl they can be sorted and restored to the tall shutters of the front windows. (Left) Tall shutter waiting to be reattached to the window frame. The green color of the shutters and the remaining white paint seen on the window is the orignal paint which has taken on a slightly lighter shade due to the ravages of the California and Georgia sun.

The photos in this chapter show a number of shutters and windows, but there were only three tall windows on Tara's front porch. Normally Southern homes were symmetrical with an equal number of windows on each side, but due to the location of the façade on the set, the filming was done on the right side of the house. The front door had to be moved to the right so it would not be behind one of the columns while filming.

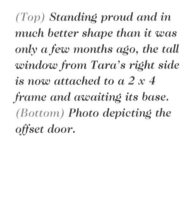

(Top) Standing proud and in much better shape than it was only a few months ago, the tall window from Tara's right side is now attached to a 2 x 4 frame and awaiting its base. (Bottom) Photo depicting the offset door.

The Official Guide to the Saving Tara Project

Mammy's Window

3

If asked to categorize which pieces of the Tara façade are most recognizable, one might put the long shot of the complete house as number one, and a close second would be the window where Mammy leaned out to chide Scarlett for "being out in the night air without a shawl" and not "asking those gentlemen to stay for supper."

Hattie McDaniel's part in *Gone With the Wind* was critical and its worth was rewarded by the Academy Award it garnered Hattie over fellow cast member Olivia de Havilland. Ms. McDaniel is beloved by all who revere the movie and her autograph is still one of the most highly sought and expensive to obtain.

So, to have the window that Hattie leaned out of to say her first lines would be a very important part of the display; but I'm afraid her window is not currently a part of the inventory. In 1989, the conservator taking the inventory reported that the window was in the possession of one who was involved in moving the façade to Coweta County, but when the deal fell through, the window was not returned with the other items.

Hattie had to stand on a ladder for this scene, since the façade had no inner finishing, much less a second floor!

The window itself is the same size (3'6" x 5') as a number of other windows that were seen in the Tara wide shot and but for the glass panes would not be distinguishable. You see, while the other 3'6" x 5' windows have "eight panes over eight," the window in question was "six panes over six." So today for the purposes of denoting size and shape I have photographed another of the 3'6" x 5' windows.

(Left) One of the large windows with one of its shutters attached. (Top right) Circled area showing "Mammy's window" as it looked during the final set dressing prior to Hattie McDaniel's appearance in it. (Middle right) Another view of the same shutter which shows the large iron hinges. All the hinges on the façade appear to be blacksmith made. (Bottom right) In order to fit each shutter correctly, the metal hooks or hangers had to be shimmed with washers so they would hang true. Here are six washers and a larger washer and bolt.

The Official Guide to the Saving Tara Project

This is a photo of the type of 3'6" x 5' window that framed Hattie McDaniel's character of Mammy in the early scenes of Gone With the Wind. At present we cannot identify the exact window used by Hattie due to damage and other factors, however there is no doubt that this is the correct size window and therfore we have a good idea of the dimensions of Tara's window.

Tara's Front Door

The front door of Tara is well known and has been well publicized since it was restored by the Tara façade's owner in 1989 and loaned for a display at the Atlanta History Center and now the Margaret Mitchell House. Thousands have gazed upon it and imagined walking thru its portal to meet the O'Haras and their eldest daughter, Scarlett.

But few realize that the entrance way presently displayed in Atlanta is a combination of the original door which was stripped down to the bare wood and a recreated door frame, sidelights, and fanlight constructed to hold the original door in place. The original pieces of the door frame and its side lights still reside in the barn no more than twenty miles south of where Margaret Mitchell wrote the novel that began it all.

Although the restored front door and its recreated framework are still the property of the façade's owners; photos of it in its present location are not included since this is a study of the pieces residing in the barn. Today those pieces are a jumble of

uprights, hinges and lock sets as well as a number of specially milled pieces that were the left overs of the wood used to replicate the front door frame now in Atlanta.

Due to the deterioration of the frame, it will never be reassembled, so posted here are photos of several pieces as well as a photo of the door on set in 1939 so that you can compare and see what pieces you recognize.

(Opposite page) Tara façade at the time of the filming, showing all the parts of its distinguishable front door. (Above) The same front door from the scene after its move to Georgia, its sale to Betty Talmadge, and loan to Atlanta History Center where it was in the process of being restored prior to display. The man standing in the door way of Tara is Atlanta Historian, the late Franklin Garrett. (Top Right) A piece of the orginal fan light replaced during the restoration. Notice the words "Tara fan light" written in red chalk. (Bottom Right) These are the frames that held the sidelights on Tara's front door during the filming. They were replaced and stored here with the rest of the façade in 1989 when the door was repaired for its display at the Atlanta History Center for the 50th Anniversary celebration of the Premier of Gone With the Wind.

A side view of veneer and molding that was replaced from the front door when it was restored. This and the other replaced pieces are stored in the dairy barn. (Top inset) A hinge and the masonite lock plate that were removed from the front door at the time of its restoration. This plate was made of the same particle board as Tara's bricks, but is less than 1/8-inch in thickness. (Bottom left inset) This cardboard box contains assorted pieces of trim that were created to replicate original pieces during the 1989 restoration in preparation for the 50th Anniversary Celebration. (Bottom right inset) These are assorted trim pieces and molding removed from Tara's front door and replaced during the 1989 restoration.

The Interior Shutters

5 Another interesting set of shutters found amongst the inventory in the dairy barn is a pair of massive interior shutters that were inside the three large front windows of Tara. In the inside shots of the O'Hara's home they are seen in the front room as Mrs. O'Hara lies in simple repose after her death, when Scarlett takes a drink as Gerald tells her of his confederate bonds and reveals he has slipped away from reality, and peeking from behind the green drapes that Scarlett plans to make into a new dress in order go to Atlanta and see Rhett for the tax money. Finally, they appear as Scarlett and Ashley discuss his leaving with Melanie and the baby to go north to seek employment.

Although the interior scenes were filmed on a sound stage and not inside of the facade, the interior shutters were also made for the façade windows. Though the interiors of the film are lost to history, we still have the interior shutters built for the facade (and painted in the same interior colors) to guide us.

The interior shutters were witness to the major events at Tara such as the unforgettable drapery to dress scene as well as Mrs. O'Hara's death (below) and Ashley's plan to leave Tara and go north (previous page).

The interior shutters languishing in the dairy barn were attached to the façade and therefore would not have been used in the shots filmed on a sound stage. But they were part of the façade and have been documented by photos taken just before the façade was dismantled and moved to Georgia. Hopefully, as we do more research into the filming, we will be better able to identify moments when these pieces were used in close ups, but until then we can say they were part of Tara and thus part of the filming and those which were used on the sound stage were twins to the ones we have today.

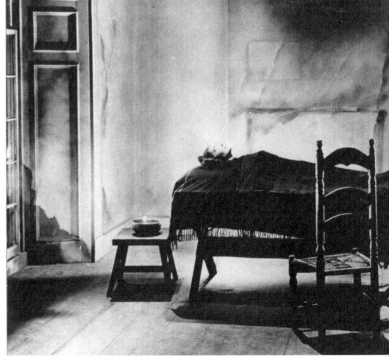

The Official Guide to the Saving Tara Project

The interior shutters look imposing and very heavy, when they are in fact light, given to their fir frame construction covered with thin oak lumber. (Inset) A close-up of the shutter and its construction as well as the myriad of cobwebs and dirt which is always a part of any restoration.

The Cathedral Window

The cathedral, or arched, window at the top of Tara's stairs was no more than a piece of the sum total of Tara walls until Scarlett (recently home from her harrowing trek from Atlanta with Melanie, baby Beau and Prissy) killed one of General Sherman's "Bummers" on the stairs. Melanie, hearing the shot, arrives dragging Charles' sword and quickly opens the curved window to assure the family who have "come a-running" that the gun shot was only an accident and since there was no harm done they should go back to their chores.

While the filming required three of the windows (one for interior shots on the sound stage, one for the exterior shot at Chico and the window attached to the façade) there appears to only be the façade window left in existence. Thus, it is another important piece of the façade to be preserved and presented for the world to see.

(Above) *This is an excellent closeup of the cathdral window as seen on the façade when shooting began.* (Top right) *The initial laying out of the larger pieces of the window served to understand its construction.* (Right) *The cathedral window is lighttly attached to a 2 x 4 frame for support until other pieces can be identified and reassembled.*

The Official Guide to the Saving Tara Project

The window standing in its support frame as work continues. Note the new wood on the left to replace a piece too badly destroyed.

This full size likeness of the Catherdral Window was created by a fan and follower of the Saving Tara Project. I hope he can be convinced to help us in restoring the original that is on display in the barn.

The Soldiers and the Side Porch

The side porch, which became a place of convalescence for the weary soldiers of the south as they stopped to beg food on their long walk home, has long been a favorite scene in the movie. It is an excellent place to study the clothing and props, and many longtime fans of Olivia de Havilland enjoy her interaction with the soldiers. So it was a treat to look amongst the pieces of the Tara façade and report that all eleven stairs, some hand rails, ceiling beams and even a portion of the cedar shake roof have survived the march of time…and termites.

The Official Guide to the Saving Tara Project

Three of the volunteers celebrate with Peter as they identify the orignal locations of the "porch posts." (Bottom left) Two of the posts showing the ghosts which are paint marks or discolorations to help in the reassembly. The arrow shaped marks show the connection of the handrails to the posts. (Bottom right) Close-up of the porch steps. Note the man-made hole that was drilled and then filled with a plug to make it appear as though these modern boards had knot holes.

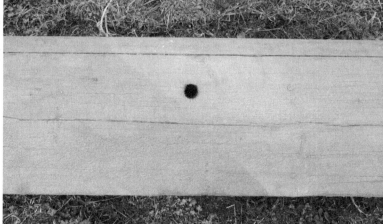

30

Upon a closer look it was found that the wide treads had holes drilled into them and then filled with a rough hand-cut wooden peg to give the look of a knot hole. The hand rails that ran the length of the porch were also found. It was at these rails that Scarlett folded a piece of clothing while hearing the news from Melly that Ashley had been taken prisoner.

Previous page: (Top left) Side view of Tara showing the side porch, rails and shingled roof. (Bottom left) Volunteers sweeping dirt and cobb webs from the pieces of the side porch. Because of their size, all the porch pieces had to be removed from the barn, cleaned, and then restacked in the barn.

(Top right) Another view of the original steps from the side porch. (Bottom right) A close up of the arrow-shaped hand rail seen on the porch posts at the top of the stairs.

The Side Porch Door

 After Scarlett returns to Tara she finds that, as she tells Mr. Frank Kennedy, she is the "head of the house now." As Scarlett moves about her beloved Tara, "trying to keep body and soul together," she finds herself walking up the steps of the side porch from the kitchen and thru the side door into the house many times as part of her daily routine.

Not long after speaking with Melanie on the side porch about Ashley's apparent capture at the battle of Spotsylvania, Scarlett walks thru the side door into the house with Mr. Kennedy (still draped in an old quilt) close on her heals as he asks permission to marry Suellen. If you pay close attention to the film you will see that as Scarlett opens the door, the film is then spliced as they cut away to a sound stage for the interior scenes.

When the set was inventoried in 1989, five doors were noted. One was the massive front door with side lights and fan light that would require restoration and even replication before it could be put on display at the Atlanta History Center. The other four doors were those from the left side porches, the breezeway

(Right) A number of the pieces of the door and large window pieces from the side door area of the side porch. (Bottom left) A close-up of the fluted post that was built three sided so it could be slipped over the 2 x 4 frame work of the façade. (Bottom right) The door itself that lead from the back hallway.

into the kitchen and, of course, the door used by Scarlett to enter the house from the right side porch landing near where the soldiers were being fed.

But this, the latter door, is even suspect. As we have sought to follow the ghost markings and reattach the pieces, some parts of the puzzle have failed to fit, no matter how hard we banged on them. There is a nagging suspicion amongst those working on the façade that the door currently identified as the side porch door, may not be so.

But this does not render the work a failure. For the goal was, and continues to be, discovery and to show that the pieces of the most iconic of all movie sets still exists and can be viewed and enjoyed by the public.

....

The door and frame attached to modern 2 x 4 framing to allow them to stand.

The Beadboard Shutters in the Background

9

An interesting piece among the items brought from Hollywood is a set of bead board shutters that still retain their rustic iron closure. These shutters, still in very good condition and retaining most of their original paint were identified only after watching the movie frame by frame.

As is the usual practice in film-making, a lot of work goes into set dressing and many times fine pieces of work become just a distant part of the back ground, or, in the case of these shutters, a fleeting second of film that is seen only by those who search for it. These shutters hung on the porch wall only a few inches from where Prissy was cutting and serving watermelon to the hungry confederate soldiers who sat eating on the steps. The only time these shutters come into view is when Melly hurries past Prissy to speak to Scarlett just before she enters the house thru the side door.

However, this fine example of Hollywood construction serves to remind us of the great care that went into the work of movies and also provides a tangible reminder, once again, of the moments when Scarlett, Melly and Prissy shared the screen.

Scrap wood is attched horizontally to keep the shutters from coming apart.

(Opposite page) *Note the overlap of the two shutters so that they close completely... some of the fine carpentry skills found among the pieces of the façade.* (Top) *The window behind the beadboard shutters is considered at this time to be the most intact of all the windows present.* (Right) *The circled area is the location of the bead board shutters and the accompanying window. Butterfly McQueen's character, "Prissy" was filmed standing near it in the scene with the soldiers eating on the side porch. Few photos exist of this window and it is therefore best seen by viewing the movie scene by scene in slow motion.*

The Official Guide to the Saving Tara Project

The window in its frame with the shutters set to the side.

The Forgotten Left Side of Tara

While some of the pieces of the Tara façade were seen in the full frontal shots of Tara as well as part of specific scenes and close ups, this was not the case for the left side of the Tara façade. The left side of the house included windows, dentil moulding and columns on a side porch which were all crafted with as much detail as the right side, without ever being filmed close up. Amongst the pieces of the façade there are windows, dentil moulding, shutters and porch pieces that show weathering but not the heavy distress of the right side that was seen in close up shots.

Even though they may not be as famous as their cousins on the other side of the house, they are still part of the Tara façade and visible in the full shots taken of the house. In fact, these left side pieces have been a major contributor in the restoration of the right side pieces as they provided a template for how the right side pieces were constructed.

(Top) The windows and their matching shutters for the left side of Tara. (Upper right) These same windows in disarray prior to being sorted. (Lower right) The columns for the left side of Tara. Compare these to Tara's right side and note distinct differences between the left and right sides. (Bottom left) Close up of dentil moulding on the bottom of left side column.

40

CPSIA information can be obtained at www.ICGtesting.com
Printed in the USA
LVOW01s1439230814

399835LV00002B/2/P